How Does the Water Cycle Affect Weather?

Houghton Mifflin Harcourt™

PHOTOGRAPHY CREDITS: COVER (bg) ©Steve Satushek/Getty Images; 3 (b) ©Brand X Pictures/Getty Images; 7 (l) ©Steve Satushek/Getty Images; 7 (cr) ©Ellen McKnight/Alamy Images; (cl) ©Andreas Riedmiller/Getty Images; (r) ©imagebroker.net/Superstock; 9 (t) ©VStock/Alamy Images; 10 (b) ©Digital Vision/Getty Images; 11 (t) ©Ilene MacDonald/ Alamy Images; 12 (b) ©Stephen St. John/National Geographic/Getty Images; 13 (t) ©MELBA PHOTO AGENCY/Alamy Images; 14 (r) ©Science & Society Picture Library/Getty Images; (l) ©Artur Synenko/Shutterstock; 15 (l) ©Alamy Images; (r) ©Raine Vara/Alamy Images; 16 (bg) ©Michael Dwyer/Alamy Images; 17 (t) ©NASA; 19 (t) ©Tetra Images/Getty Images; 20 (b) ©Laralova/Shutterstock; 21 (bg) ©InterNetwork Media/Digital Vision/Getty Images

Printed in the U.S.A.

ISBN: 978-0-544-07308-1

12 13 14 15 16 17 18 19 20 1083 20 19 18

4500710587   A B C D E F G

uk for each word in yellow along with its meaning.

water cycle	precipitation	humidity
evaporation	groundwater	air pressure
atmosphere	runoff	air mass
condensation	weather	front

 Underlined sentences answer the questions.

What is the water cycle?

What happens during the water cycle?

Why does it rain?

How does water move?

What is weather?

What are the properties of weather?

Which tools do scientists use to measure weather?

How do scientists track weather?

What are air masses?

How do scientists predict weather?

What is the water cycle?

About three-fourths of Earth is covered with water. Most of the water is in the oceans. Some is in rivers, lakes, and streams. Water is also in the air and under the ground. It is even in plants and in our bodies.

The water on Earth is always moving. It moves from the surface of Earth to the air above. It also moves to the ground below. Wind and clouds move water in the air. As it moves, the water changes form. It changes from a liquid to a solid or gas.

All of these things happen in the water cycle. <u>The water cycle is the process by which water keeps moving from Earth's surface into the atmosphere and back again.</u> Let's find out more about the water cycle.

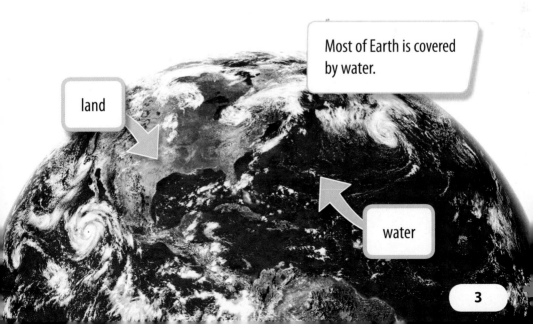

Most of Earth is covered by water.

land

water

What happens during the water cycle?

The water cycle makes it possible for water to be used over and over again.

Water collects on Earth in many different places. When it rains, lakes and rivers fill up with rainwater. Water soaks into the soil and moves underground. Plants soak up water through their roots.

Sunlight warms Earth and heats the water. The heated water changes from a liquid form to water vapor. Water vapor is an invisible gas. The process by which liquid water changes to water vapor is evaporation. Water evaporates from Earth's surface. It evaporates from oceans and lakes, from the leaves of plants, and even from underground.

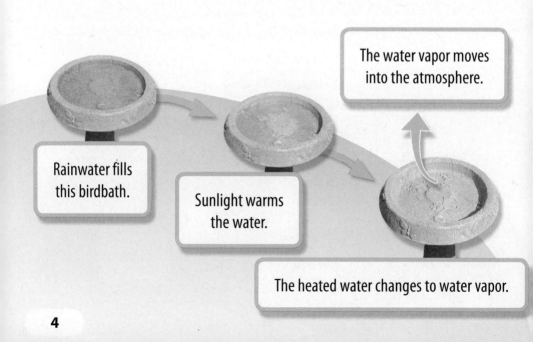

Rainwater fills this birdbath.

Sunlight warms the water.

The heated water changes to water vapor.

The water vapor moves into the atmosphere.

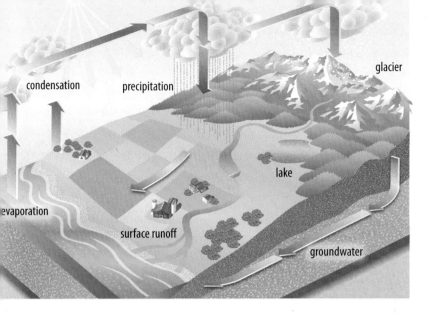

condensation precipitation glacier

lake

evaporation

surface runoff

groundwater

Water moves from Earth's surface into the atmosphere and back again. This is the water cycle.

Water vapor moves up into the atmosphere. The atmosphere is the mixture of gases that surrounds Earth. As water vapor moves, it loses heat. It cools and becomes liquid water again. This is condensation. Condensation is the process by which a gas changes to a liquid.

After a while, the liquid falls back to Earth, and the water cycle starts again. How do you think water falls back to Earth?

Why does it rain?

The atmosphere contains tiny particles, or bits of matter. Water vapor cools and mixes with these particles in the atmosphere to form tiny drops of water. Many, many drops come together to form clouds.

Clouds may cover about three-fifths of Earth's surface. Some clouds form high in the sky. Others form low, near Earth's surface. A low-forming cloud is called fog.

Water cools and mixes with small particles to form a tiny drop.

Many drops gather together in a cloud to form one drop of rain.

rain

sleet

hail

snow

Precipitation is water that falls as rain, sleet, snow, or hail.

Blasts of air keep the tiny drops of water floating. More and more tiny drops of water gather to form clouds. When the drops of water become heavy, they fall back to Earth. Precipitation is water that falls from clouds to Earth's surface. Rain, snow, sleet, and hail are all forms of precipitation.

Rain is liquid water that falls from clouds. Snow forms as pieces of ice when temperatures are cold. Sleet forms when water freezes before it hits the ground. Hail forms in several steps. First, water drops rise up and freeze into drops of ice. Then the wind blows them. As the icy drops rise and fall, layers of ice stick to them. This can happen many times until the icy pieces become heavy and drop to Earth as hail.

How does water move?

Where does precipitation go? Much of it goes into oceans and lakes. It also forms puddles on the ground. Then, when sun heats the water, it evaporates and goes back into the atmosphere. Evaporation is one way that water moves.

Another way that water moves is by soaking into the ground and becoming groundwater. Groundwater is water that is located below Earth's surface. The water is found within gaps between bits of soil. It is also found within pores in rocks. Groundwater can be near Earth's surface. It can also be deep below. Groundwater can come up to the surface and form natural springs.

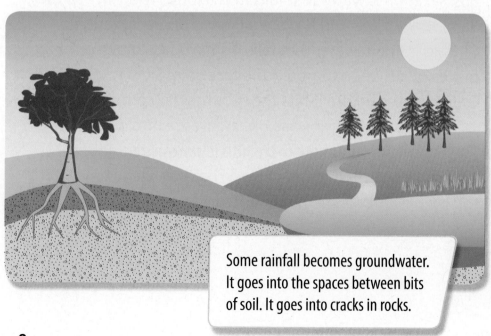

Some rainfall becomes groundwater. It goes into the spaces between bits of soil. It goes into cracks in rocks.

Heavy rainstorms can cause lakes, rivers, and streams to flood.

Water also moves as runoff. Runoff is water that doesn't soak into the ground. Instead, it flows across Earth's surface. Some of the water flows into lakes, rivers, and streams. Flooding occurs if the lakes, rivers, and streams get too high. Flooding can also happen in lowland areas.

Have you ever seen a glacier in a movie or a television show? Glaciers are very large frozen masses of water. When they melt, they leave runoff. The runoff may flow into oceans. Sometimes it can form new lakes. It may also become groundwater. Glacial melting is another way that water moves.

What is weather?

You have probably asked the question, "What's the weather like today?" People often ask this question. They want to know if it will be hot or cold. They want to know if it will rain or snow.

The weather affects what we do. We might want to go swimming. We have to find out if it is warm enough to swim. We want to know if we should bring an umbrella to school. We want to find out if it's cold enough to wear a jacket, gloves, or boots.

What is weather? Weather is what is happening in the atmosphere at a certain place and time.

We check the weather before we play outdoor sports.

Weather reports tell us if it will be cold or hot.

Earth's atmosphere is a mixture of gases. These gases include water vapor, nitrogen, oxygen, and carbon dioxide. The movement of the gases in the atmosphere creates weather. Weather happens in the part of the atmosphere that is closest to Earth's surface.

Listen to a weather report. You will hear words such as *air temperature*, *humidity*, and *air pressure*. What do these words mean? What do they have to do with weather?

11

What are the properties of weather?

Air temperature, humidity, and air pressure are the main properties of weather. Let's start with air temperature. Air temperature is how warm or cool the air is. We use a thermometer to measure air temperature. Do you know the air temperature where you are right now? Is it warmer or cooler than yesterday?

Humidity is the amount of water vapor in the air. A lot of water vapor means the humidity is high. High humidity makes the air feel damp. Little water vapor means the humidity is low. Then the air feels dry. If the air temperature is warm, the air can hold more water vapor. If the air temperature is cold, it can hold less water vapor.

A thermometer measures air temperature. It shows how warm or cool it is outside.

low air pressure

Air pressure at sea level is greater than the air pressure in the mountains.

high air pressure

Humidity affects the amount of precipitation that falls. When the humidity is high, there is a better chance of precipitation. If the air is warm, it could rain. If the air is cold, it could snow.

Did you know that air presses down on you? Air pressure is the weight of the atmosphere pressing down on Earth's surface. Temperature and humidity both affect air pressure. When the air is cold, the air pressure is higher. When the air is warm, the air pressure is lower. Humid air has less air pressure than dry air. Air pressure gets lower as elevation, or height above sea level, rises.

Air pressure changes. When it changes, the weather is also likely to change. Let's find out how scientists measure air pressure.

Which tools do scientists use to measure weather?

Scientists use a barometer to measure air pressure. One type of barometer is a mercury barometer. It is made of a bowl containing mercury and a long glass tube. The tube is about 76 centimeters (30 inches) long. One end of the tube is closed and the other is open. The open end is placed into the bowl. When the air pressure is high, the mercury moves up into the tube. When air pressure is low, the mercury moves down.

Another type of barometer is an aneroid barometer. It has a cylinder with springs inside. The cylinder is made of metal that bends easily. Air is taken out of the cylinder. The air pressure causes the cylinder to either get larger or smaller. Then, the springs move a pointer on a dial. The pointer shows the amount of air pressure.

aneroid barometer

mercury barometer

anemometer

The cups on this anemometer spin on a windy day.

wind vane

A wind vane shows the direction of the wind.

What is wind? Wind is the movement of air from places with higher pressure to places with lower pressure. This movement is a bit like water flowing downhill. Scientists can measure the speed of wind with a tool called an anemometer.

Look at the picture of the anemometer above. Wind pushes on the cups at the top of an anemometer. This causes them to spin. The anemometer measures how fast the cups move. This tells the wind speed.

Another wind tool is a wind vane. This tool shows the direction from which the wind blows.

How do scientists track weather?

Scientists called meteorologists have different ways to track, or follow, weather. At sea, scientists use weather buoys to collect data. These buoys measure air temperature, air pressure, and wind direction. They also measure water temperature and the height of the waves. People who live on the coast need this weather information.

On land, scientists get weather information from weather-monitoring stations. These stations have tools that gather data about the atmosphere. They can track the weather conditions in near and faraway places. They can also warn people about storms that might be coming. These stations may have tools like Doppler radar towers, which can observe movements and changes in storm clouds.

People on boats can call the Dial-a-Buoy number. The information helps them decide if it's safe to go out on the water.

44013

NOAA

TIROS-1

This is the first weather satellite. It was sent into space in 1960. It improved weather forecasting.

Scientists learn about the weather from weather balloons and weather satellites high above Earth. Weather balloons carry a tool called a *radiosonde*. This tool measures air temperature, humidity, and air pressure.

Weather satellites travel around Earth. They collect data about weather. They can track weather over large areas, such as storms and hurricanes. They can measure cloud cover. Satellites use radio signals to send this information to Earth. Weather satellites can also pick up information from weather tools on land.

What are air masses?

Sometimes the weather will change suddenly. Did you ever wonder why? It could have something to do with an air mass. An air mass is a large body of air with the same temperature and humidity throughout. An air mass can form over land or water. An air mass has a temperature and humidity similar to the temperature and humidity of the land or water over which it forms. Air masses that form over land are dry. Air masses that form over oceans are damp.

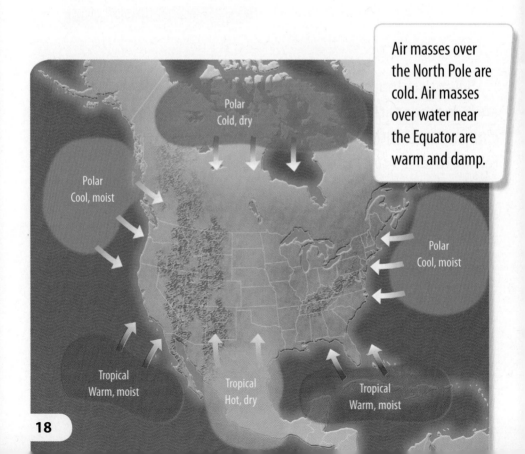

Air masses over the North Pole are cold. Air masses over water near the Equator are warm and damp.

Polar
Cold, dry

Polar
Cool, moist

Polar
Cool, moist

Tropical
Warm, moist

Tropical
Hot, dry

Tropical
Warm, moist

Do you want to see how two air masses meet? Open a clothes dryer after it has stopped. Feel the warm air come into the cooler room.

Two air masses can move and bump into each other. The place where they meet is called a front. For example, a cold air mass might pass over a place that has been warm. The cold air takes the place of the warmer air. This is called a cold front. Then the temperature goes down. This change explains why the air temperature might be warm one day and cool the next.

Weather changes happen because of the movement of air masses and fronts. But how can scientists tell when these changes will happen?

How do scientists predict weather?

A weather forecast tells what the weather of a place might be. Weather forecasts are in newspapers. They're also on TV, radio, and the Internet. Forecasts tell what the weather will be like tomorrow. They can sometimes tell what it will be like next week, too!

As you've learned, meteorologists are scientists who track and tell about the weather. Meteorologists use tools such as buoys, balloons, and Doppler radar. They use these tools to learn about air temperature, humidity, and air pressure. They look at the movement of air masses and fronts, too. They analyze this information on computers. Then they use computer programs to make weather maps.

weather forecast

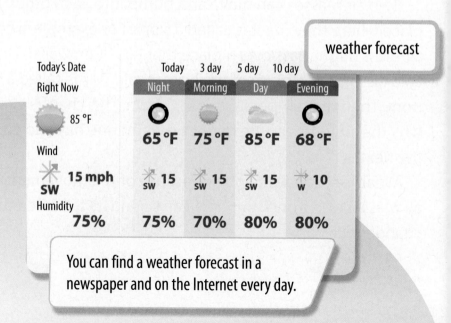

Today's Date Right Now		Today	3 day	5 day	10 day
		Night	Morning	Day	Evening
	85 °F	65 °F	75 °F	85 °F	68 °F
Wind	15 mph SW	SW 15	SW 15	SW 15	W 10
Humidity	75%	75%	70%	80%	80%

You can find a weather forecast in a newspaper and on the Internet every day.

This is a picture of a hurricane. Meteorologists use satellites to locate storms and hurricanes.

Meteorologists use computers to share weather information. They send it to other scientists all over the world. Meteorologists also use computers to make weather models. These models tell about big weather events, such as hurricanes.

Scientists in the United States use weather satellites to get information. They have been doing this for more than 50 years. Satellites pick up information from faraway places on Earth. This helps scientists do a better job of telling about weather changes. Scientists can also use satellites to track events such as hurricanes. They can find out how fast a storm moves and how strong it is. This helps people prepare for storms. The information can save lives.

Measure Rainfall with a Rain Gauge

Work with a partner. Gather these materials: a large plastic cup, a ruler, and tape. Tape the ruler to the inside edge of the cup. Place the cup outside in a place where it will catch rainfall. Each day, look to see if there is liquid in the cup. Measure the liquid in the cup. Record the amount of liquid for each day in a chart. Do this every day for a month.

At the end of the month, use the information to make a bar graph. Use the bar graph to answer these questions: Which day had the most rain? Which had the least rain? How much rain fell this month?

Write About Weather Tools

Choose one of the weather tools you learned about. Make a poster about this tool. Find or draw a picture of the tool. Write labels for parts of the tool. Write a caption telling about this weather tool. Include information about what the tool does, where it works, and why it is important.

Glossary

air mass [AIR MAS] A large body of air that has the same temperature and humidity throughout. *A warm, damp air mass is moving across the ocean and coming to our area.*

air pressure [AIR PRESH•er] The weight of the atmosphere pressing down on Earth. *The air pressure is lower in the mountains.*

atmosphere [AT•muhs•feer] The mixture of gases that surrounds Earth. *Rain and snow form in the atmosphere.*

condensation [kahn•duhn•SAY•shuhn] The process by which a gas changes into a liquid. *You can see condensation on the outside of this ice-filled glass.*

evaporation [ee•vap•uh•RAY•shuhn] The process by which a liquid changes into a gas. *Evaporation has made the water on the grass disappear.*

front [FRUHNT] The boundary between two air masses. *A cold front moved in, so it will be chilly soon.*

groundwater [GROWND•waw•ter] Water located within gaps and pores in rocks below Earth's surface. *Dig a hole in the sand near the ocean and you'll find groundwater!*

humidity [hyoo·MID·uh·tee] The amount of water vapor in the air. *When the humidity is high, you may feel damp and sticky.*

precipitation [pree·sip·uh·TAY·shuhn] Water that falls from clouds to Earth's surface. *The children were disappointed when the precipitation turned from snow to rain.*

runoff [RUN·awf] Water that does not soak into the ground and instead flows across Earth's surface. *The runoff from a stream flowed right across the park.*

water cycle [WAWT·er SY·kuhl] The process in which water continuously moves from Earth's surface into the atmosphere and back again. *Water keeps changing form during the water cycle.*

weather [WETH·er] What is happening in the atmosphere at a certain place and time. *This week's weather will have warm temperatures, high pressure, and low humidity.*